HEALING - THE SHAMAN'S WAY

Norman W. Wilson PhD

HEALING - THE SHAMAN'S WAY

Cover Design by

www.srwalkerdesigns.com

Interior Photography by
Suzanne V. Wilson Photography

A ZADKIEL PUBLISHING PAPERBACK

ISBN: 978-1-78695-163-2

Zadkiel Publishing
An Imprint of Fiction4All
www.fiction4all.com

This Edition
Published 2018

In memory of Elisapie

I will respect the privacy of my clients, for their problems are not disclosed to me that the world may know. Most especially must I tread with care in matters of life and death. Above all, I must not play at God.

From a modern version of the Hippocratic Oath

PREFACE

The intent of this book is not to make you a healing practitioner, but rather, to provide you fundamental information that will help you better understand what it is that a shaman does. I feel this becomes especially important in today's setting with the increase in the number of persons claiming to be shamans, shamanic practitioners, and shamanic weavers. Second, I feel there are things that one may do to help heal him or herself. These should not be kept secret.

My advice, as always, is to communicate your intent to try a complimentary or supportive healing approach with your medical doctor. Real integrative medicine is in a watershed moment.

If herbs and herbals are suggested for your use, make sure you have no allergies that might be negatively impacted by such medicinal herbal treatment. Know your blood pressure because some suggested shamanic treatments might be an impediment. The herbs I have suggested are quite common, but still, prudence is the best policy to follow.

DISCLAIMER

I do not guarantee that any of the suggestions presented in this book will work, cure any physical or psychological issues, or enhance anyone's living conditions. Each person must make that choice for her or himself.

Age has no reality except in the physical world. The essence of a human being is resistant to the passage of time. Our inner lives are eternal, which is to say that our spirits remain as

as when we were in full bloom. Think of love as a state of grace, not the means to anything but the alpha and omega. An end in itself.

Gabriel Garcia Marques
Love in the Time of Cholera

SHAMANISM IS NOT A RELIGION

TABLE OF CONTENTS

I - ORIGINS

What is the origin of the word shaman (pronounced SHAY-man or SHA-man)? There is some disagreement over the actual origin of the word. Some scholars claim the word shamanism is so indiscriminately used, it no longer has meaning. And there are those who claim a complete definition is impossible. Two Dutch diplomats who accompanied Peter the Great's emissaries to China during the late Seventeenth Century are credited with first using the term, shaman.

In 1875, the Encyclopedia Britannica published an article by A.H. Sayee, which used the word *shaman*. Opinion indicates the word is of Tungas origin. More specifically, it appears that the term came from the Manchu-tangu dialect of Siberia, from where we derive our most common usage.

However, even this is not without challenge. Some ethnolinguists claim the word derives from the Chinese *scha-man*, while others claim it's from the Pali *schamana*, a term used for a Buddhist monk. There does appear to be common agreement that the word shaman came into modern language from the Sanskrit, *sramana.*

The word shamanism, which has been around since the 1600s has now become a universally recognized term in Western Culture and refers to a man or woman who fills several roles within the culture. Specifically, two aspects of shamanism have gained popularity: physical and psychological healing. [1]

Because the word *shaman* has become a part of our popular vocabulary and is understood to be someone who is a healer, I choose to use it. However, it needs to be said that not all Native Americans like the term. It is not a part of the languages of the many Native American tribes. My use of the word *shaman* is not intended to be an insult.

In my book *Shamanism What It's All About* I briefly talk about my initiation and in my novels, I reveal more of those details. Even though I have been hesitant to claim I am a shaman I suppose now that I am nearing my senior years of life in this dimension, I no longer feel the need to concern myself with the stigma of being "different." As it says in the Hebrew Bible, "ehyeh asher ehyeh," which when translated in the King James Version as "I am that I am."

My initiation into the world of shamanic healing was by a group of the Mi'kmaq. The Mi'kmaq live in Nova Scotia, Prince Edward Island, New Brunswick, the Gaspe Peninsula of Quebec Province and the state of Maine. And especially by my beloved Elisapie. In English her name is Elizabeth.

The Mi'kmaq are a fascinating indigenous people. Strange as it may seem, these native people gave the French the name *nikmaq*, meaning "my kind friends." The early French explorers and settlers, in turn, gave these natives the very name they had been called. The Mi'kmaq are a part of the larger group called Algonquian.

It is said the Mi'kmaq lived in the forested areas of Canada for over 2,000 years. Some say it is more likely 10,000 years. Even though they were decimated by the Indian Wars and disease during the 18th Century, there are those who did survive and their descendants continue to provide us important linkage in our world today.

Originally, the Mi'kmaq were a society that lived in small villages of about one hundred families. They were a patrilineal group, that is, the son inherited from the father.

The number seven is very important in the Mi'kmaq culture. They divided their living area into seven distinct areas. A male member of the group represented each area, giving the governing council seven members. Their most powerful "spirit medicine" was made of seven barks and roots.

Admirably, the Mi'kmaq respected and feared the natural world, believing they were dependent upon the good will of their prey, and further, that all animals once held human form. Consequently, the animals were given supernatural powers and created a world of spirits. They believed that the spirit of a dead animal killed during the hunt watched the hunter, making sure that its bones were well treated. The bones of a fish, for example, had to be put back into the stream or lake from which it was taken.

A rare few of the Mi'kmaq developed certain innate abilities that allowed them to surpass all others in their perceptions, skills, and talents. They had special powers. I suspect that they had fine-tuned their ability to tie into what is now called the Non-local mind [2]. Additionally, I believe they were adept at reading auras, thus giving them indications of a person's health. Such persons often had to pay a high price for being different. These few gifted were often separated from the rest of the tribe, frequently living in deep forested areas, isolated and sometimes feared; coming into the village to seek a mate, or for a sacred ritual they were called upon to preform, to use their magical powers to heal the sick, or to make predictions.

If I recall correctly, my parents met some Mi'kmaqs during their first visit to the Baskatong in 1939. They had gone into the "bush" with another couple for a two-week fishing trip. I stayed home. We had a "hired girl" who took care of me. She was never referred to as a servant and never treated in a way other than as part of our family. I made my first trip into the Canadian bush the spring of 1940. That summer I would turn seven years old. I would spend every summer there for the next fourteen years of my life.

The Baskatong, located in western Quebec Province, Canada, is a man-made lake formed by the construction of Mercier Dam in 1927. The lake has an area of 268 miles. The word wild is a good word to describe the area.

Sometimes we arrived in the middle of May or early June. I preferred later in June because there were fewer mosquitoes. But then, I had nothing to say about the matter.

May was definitely a time for those pesky and nasty insects. They seemed especially attracted to me. An Indian woman named Elisapie who lived in one of the three wigwams gave me a flowering plant to rub on my skin. When I asked where I could find such a plant she pointed to the large field between her wigwam and our log cabin. It was, as I learned later, called horsemint (See photo below). I picked a lot of that plant over the years. I would crush the leaves and flowers in my hand and rub it on my skin. It smelled like Greek Oregano. The mosquitoes did not like its smell and left me alone, for which I was eternally grateful.

II - ON THE BASKATONG

The whole area called the Baskatong was a pristine slice of natural wonderment. Massive stands of wooded areas of evergreens, oak, maple, and white birch populated the area. Wild flowers such as daisies, sage, thistle, prickly rose, poppies, and strawflowers created a living Monet. Sweet wild huckleberries were always welcome and were enjoyed not only by me but also by bears, especially brown bears. As a consequence, I was always warned to be on the lookout whenever I went berry picking. Occasionally, in what became known as "the field," I would spot a moose enjoying its breakfast.

Our log cabin, with its dirt floor, one window with gauze for a screen, sat quite some distance from the row of three wigwams that housed members of Mi'kmaq Tribe.

The lone window, in our log

cabin, facing south, had a wooden door we closed at night to keep out wild animals. We had no inside plumbing. There was two-hole outhouse some distance from our cabin where we were expected to relieve ourselves. Peeing in the lake was not acceptable. Often times, it was occupied by small mice who scurried away as soon as the door was unlatched. One time we ran out of toilet paper and thanks to Elisapie we quickly learned which plant to use. (Lamb's Ear) For our drinking water, my mother and I took a bucket and went into the deep woods to a natural spring. Once I learned the way, getting water was my daily chore. There I cleared away water bugs, mosquitos, and any leaves before using a dipper to fill my bucket. For dishes and laundry, my mother used lake water. We bathed in the lake, also.

I didn't know who built the cabin and the outhouse. My second summer there, a small roofless porch on the front had been added. I do remember stopping in a small town called Maniwaki and my father would talk to some man, give him some money and a bottle of whiskey. I assume he was the man who cut the wood, stacked blocks of ice and covered them with sawdust for our use. Maybe he put the porch on the cabin. It was just one or two steps up from the ground.

Depending on what time we arrived in May or June, the space between our cabin and the wigwams was filled with a massive blanket of flowers. Sometimes, if there had been a heavy winter, ice would still be on the lake and heavy clothing would be required.

As I said, my father had arranged to have a large stack of cut logs placed along one side of the cabin and covered with a tarp. We always had a fire in the potbelly stove that sat in the very center of the room. My mother cooked our meals on that legless leftover from another era. Using it, she even made a cake for my seventh birthday.

Despite the mosquitoes and sometimes very cold early springs, it was a fabulous place for the adventurous mind of a seven year old, one who fearlessly wandered into the deep woods, explored large boulders, climbed stately pines, or stole a nap in an open field. Why would I be afraid, after all, I listened to Tom Mix and The Lone Ranger on the radio. They were always around to save people, weren't they?

Wolves ran deer at night and bears rubbed their backs along the logs of our cabin, and the strange crying sounds of loons trying to take off from the lake on foggy mornings woke me. There were long days of fishing for Great Northern and Walleye or wandering along the miles of sandy lake shore. Despite the fact there were no other children there, I never felt lonely. One reason was Elisapie [3]. More about her later.

Once in a rare while, we were treated by an airplane of the Royal Canadian Airforce swooping down low over the lake and our cabin. Once, the plane was so low I could see the pilot's face. He waved back at me as I waved at him.

Directly across from our one-room cabin was a small island whose top was snow white. When I first saw it, I was sure it was snow. It was not. It was white quartz. I still have a piece sitting on my bookcase. I had a small one man rowboat and the island, my island as it came to exist in my mind, was a favorite haunt. At age seven and weighing in at not quite fifty pounds, it took me about twenty minutes to row over to my island. Since I could not swim, a life jacket was mandatory as well as a floating cushion. Despite that fact, I was not afraid nor did my parents seem overly concerned about my being out by myself.

Sometimes, I'd put the oars down and just let the boat drift, as I lazily watched all sorts of cloud formations, giant animals mostly. A face would appear and tease me into a fantasy at least I thought it was a fantasy. I know better now. Sometimes there would be several beings all different from the pictures of angels I had seen in church school. But then, who is to say? My mother always made sure I had some kind of a snack. If I got thirsty, I simply cupped my hand, leaned over the boat and scooped up water from the lake.

I won't go into some of the details of my "initiation" because I have written about them in other books. Elisapie, whom I called Sa-pie (Say Pie) and I became great friends. Grandmotherly best describes her and despite her weathered brown skin and toothless smile, her eyes betrayed her age. They not only sparkled but they seemed to dance in deliberate opposition to her boney body. She wasn't very tall, not as tall as my mother who claimed to be five feet. If we stood back to back, she might have been a quarter of a head taller than me. She always wore a necklace that had a black figure attached to it. I asked her about it. She said it was the head of a blackbird.

Once, just as the dawn broke open I watched her paddle out in her birch bark canoe, headed north. She had four dogs with her. They were loud noisy barkers. They became instantly quiet when she raised one finger. A couple of hours later she returned. The dogs jumped from the canoe and raced toward the wigwams, delighted to be back on solid ground. Say-pie seemed to struggle to get the canoe up on land. I was about to go and help her when a man appeared. He bent down, lifted something out of the canoe. It was a deer. That surprised me. My mother hunted but never alone. Say-Pie looked up, saw me, and waved for me to join them.

I brought back a good-sized piece of venison to my mother. It was good eating. She pounded it with a saucer, added flour, salt, and pepper. She cooked it in bacon fat.

On the days when I was not fishing with my parents or wandering around my island, Say-Pie took me for long walks in the woods and fields. As we walked, me in moccasins she made for me from elk's skin, she pointed out wild plants she said were good to eat. She showed me wapato, sometimes called arrowhead. Its tubers were like potatoes. Wild asparagus seemed to be one of her favorites. She used it to make a fritter for me to eat. When she showed me catnip I thought she was joking. Say-Pie pointed out that it was good for several things: Catnip is used if you have trouble sleeping, used for headaches, colds, and indigestion.

Other plants she identified as good medicine and bad medicine.

I quickly learned which plants were bad medicine: poison ivy (that's a story for another time), poison oak, nettles, bloodroot, and water hemlock.

One year when we returned to our cabin, Say-Pie and her group were not there. I never saw her again. Even though I was heartbroken, I kept my disappointment to myself. Often, her face comes to me in my dreams. I always see her dancing eyes and I hear her softly saying, almost under her breath, "Nepiteget," meaning healer.

Because of a lack of use, much of what she taught has gone by the wayside. Every once-in-awhile something will jog my memory and I will recall something that happened during those years. For example, my vision quest gift.

After my quest, Say-Pie presented me with a white birch bark canoe, showed me what to do if I tipped over. She had attached a vine rope the full length of the canoe and on both sides. "Grab on to that and push toward shore." Shaking her gnarled fingers at me, she scolded, "Don't try to tip the canoe back over. All you will do is sink it. You'll be in big trouble." She knew I could not swim. I haven't been in a canoe since my last stay on the Baskatong

Today, there are available excellent books, videos and television programs to help one learn the natural world. Even so, it is always wise to have someone with you who is an expert in identifying plants in the wild.

A gentle reminder, knowledge of wild plants, animals, and the ebb and tide of the seasons does not make one a shaman. However, such knowledge certainly is helpful in the treatment of clients.

III - ON BECOMING A SHAMANIC HEALER

In my book, *Shamanism What It's All About,* I go into some detail on how one becomes a shaman. There, I list seven ways through which one may become a shaman: passing on, life-threatening, display of special and unique skills, have a trainer, spiritual visitation, deprivation or isolation, and or going into an altered state of consciousness. Actually, a combination of these could be used. I am not going into a detailed account of these approaches here.

To begin, I want to comment about the term *shamanic healer.* From my perspective, it is redundant. The word shaman means healer. I think the term is confused with the *shamanic practitioner*, a term used by moderns who use healing techniques from the past and from current indigenous peoples of the world. This does not suggest that such healing is diminished but as with everything else, it depends on the competency of the individual(s) involved. The late Michael Harner has done much to bring back and preserve many of the shamanic techniques. [4]

The second point I want to make at this time is that shaman and or other healers do not actually do the healing. They function as a conduit for universal energy, life-force, or prana to seamlessly flow to the client. From my point of view, anyone who claims they do the healing should be held suspect. Such a concern becomes all the more important in today's world in which there appears to be an increasing proliferation of "shamanic healers".

My third point concerns the use of hallucinogens. Drugs which bring about a trance are used by some of the indigenous peoples of the world; not all do. People have died when they have been given some of the drugs to create "dream time." In addition to that concern, I feel that if one is hallucinating when traveling to another realm to seek the help of the spiritual world one must be in control. There is just too great a chance that messages from the spirits would be missed or misunderstood. That could cause irreparable harm to a client or even death.

Some of my shaman friends and shamanic practitioners disagree with me and I respect their experience but decline to knowingly participate in the use of such drugs.

A fourth point concerns the general field of shamanic healing. Each healer has her or his own techniques, approaches, and favorites. There is no standardization. Fees charged vary as widely as do healing approaches. For example, one of my shaman friends charges $15,000 dollars to work with a client. That charge includes working with another shaman who lives in the Amazon.

I believe I was selected to be a shaman. I prefer not to use the word chosen because it has religious and historical connotations I do not believe apply to me. And as the years have come and gone I have realized Say-Pie's wild asparagus pancakes induced dreaming; actually were helpful in my controlling my lucid dreams. At that time, I did not know or understand what lucid dreaming was. I just knew their reality. This is not a contradiction to my belief in the use of hallucinogens. My understanding of the use of wild asparagus is not to induce trance.

Because of my age, turning seven that first summer, my vision quest was different from those I now know about. Some quests last several days with the individual being deprived of water and food, and sometimes shelter. This produces a trance-like state. In *Shamanism What It's All About,* I include a photograph of myself sitting on the rock where I stayed during my vision quest. The photo was not taken during the quest but sometime later.

I am sure people reading this will wonder where my parents were and why they allowed me to be initiated and to go on a vision quest. My actual initiation took place on the one day my parents went to the nearest town for supplies. It was a 140 mile round trip over animal trails, open fields, and dirt paths. I put up a fuss and was allowed to stay with Say-Pie. It was during that time that I was initiated. [5] The mark on my arm where she cut me to get a small flow of blood is now barely visible, but I know it is there. She held my arm over a small fire and let one drop at a time of blood spill into the burning embers. She placed a moist leaf on my cut. Later she told me it was yarrow.

Because of long sleeve shirts, my parents were not aware of my cut.

I am sure you think this is a bit much, but not for any American boy who listened to Tom Mix, and The Lone Ranger on the radio and watched Roy Rogers and

Dale Evans, Gene Autry, Red Ryder at the local movie theater. It was a dream made in Heaven.

Say-Pie said I had to stay on top of a large boulder. At night it would be surrounded by the tide coming in and I would not be able to get back to shore. I agreed to stay on the rock, alone and all night without telling my parents. Secrets were so much fun, especially if it was a secret kept from one's parents. I agreed to this knowing I could not swim. My parents returned the same day they left. That night I slipped out of our cabin and ran to "my" rock. The water wasn't high yet; just up to my knees so I was able to wade out to it. In June the temperature drops to a chilly 45 degrees. The warming during the day heated the rock and it kept me reasonably warm. Despite its hard surface, I laid on my back. The swirl of stars, some shooting across the wide circular expanse before me, and the Northern Lights kept me company. The far-off hoot of an owl was a further reminder I was not alone. I did that each night for three nights. I nearly got caught by my mother when I slipped back into our cabin just at daybreak. I pretended I had been to the outhouse. She didn't notice my wet feet. Fortunately, I had rolled up my pant legs so they weren't wet.

During the three nights on my rock, I had some wild dreams. Even now, I am not sure that they were dreams, maybe, just maybe, I had travelled to another dimension—and there met myself. Today I understand the concepts of doppelganger and homunculus but at that time it was just me watching me.

Recently I have noted a number of people saying they have done their Vision Quest and that makes them a shaman. Doing a Vision Quest does not make you a shaman. That is not the purpose of such a quest.

I have quoted Medicine Grizzlybear Lake before, but his comments about vision quests are so appropriate that they deserve repeating here. He says, "It is through the vision quest that we get our power. Through the vision quest, we can discover who we really are." [6]

My Rock and Me

IV - SHAMANIC TOOLS

Shaman of old used some “tools” of the trade that have moved forward in time to be used by modern shamanic healers. Please keep in mind not all healers use every one of the following. I begin with the visible accoutrements.

Often, the healer wore rattles tied around his or her ankles. As the shaman danced they added further vibration essential for healing. The sound comingled with the sound of the feet and produced a soothing experience for the client.

Adding to the sound, the shaman used gourd rattles; shaking these in a rhythmic pattern with his or her dancing. The rattles were shaken in a steady beat over the client’s body, starting at the feet and working toward the head. Here is a rattle made for me by Randy Two-Eagles Billings.

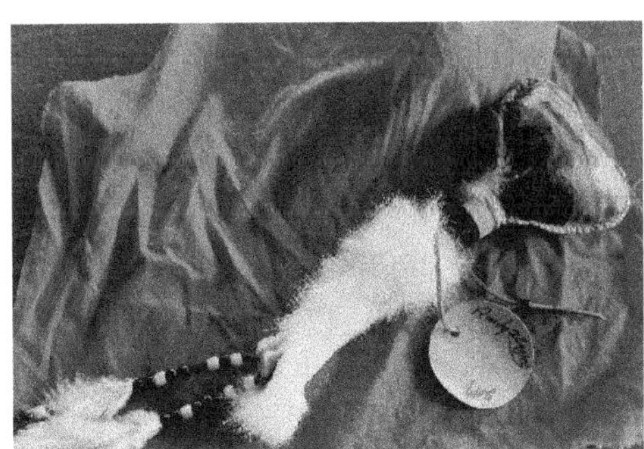

The flute, made of wood, had two functions: played around and over the client’s body to change the vibrational sequence, and to appease the Spirits. The drum, however, is the most significant of the vibrational tools. The drum and the shaman share a unique relationship, one of considerable power.

The drum, as do the flute and rattle, has two very significant functions. First, it is used to change the vibrational level of the client. In today's world, we know this is what helps the healing processes. More will be said about vibration in Chapter IX. The second function of the drums is to put the shaman in a trance state—an altered state of consciousness during which time he or she travels to another realm seeking help for the client. Michael Drake in *The Shamanic Drum A Guide to Sacred Drumming* [7] states "Drumming offers a relatively easy means of controlled transcendence." By this, he means we are able to go beyond what we perceive as ordinary reality. If the shaman intends to travel to a different realm, a separate person will do the drumming.

Basically, three types of drums that may be used by a shaman during a healing session. The first, and most common is a single-headed drum. (The photo is a single-headed drum and it is the one I currently use. By the way, it is not made of animal skin. [8]). The single-headed drum, traditionally, is a circular drum with an animal hide stretched on just one side. [9]

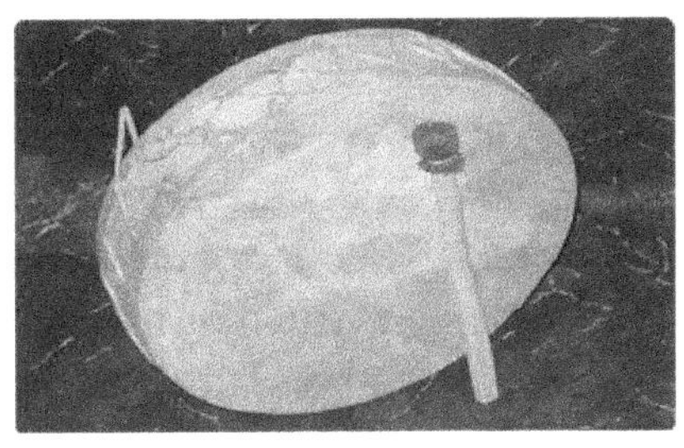

The second type of drum is the double-headed drum or hoop-drum has both sides covered with animal skin or a synthetic. This drum is often used during a sweat lodge as well as for individual healing sessions. The sound resonates beautifully between the two sides.

The third type of drum and one that is not played by the shaman is the kettle drum. It is a round drum with skin across the top. Originally, these were made from a hollowed-out log. The shaman's helper plays the kettle drum. Some Native Americans refer to the drums as "grandfather." It is a sign of deep respect. Traditionally as well as today, this drum is used to move the shaman into a hypnotic trance from which he or she will travel to one of the three realms seeking help for the client. This drum as wonderful vibrational qualities and is excellent in changing the vibrational flow in one's body.

We always need to keep in mind the power of the drum. At a talk I gave about shamanic healing, I used a one-sided drum as part of my demonstration. As I walked between the rows of attendees I realized that the sound was hypnotizing some of those present. I struck the drum faster and brought them back. Since there wasn't a deep hypnotism or at least a long lasting one I abated concern about people driving. The collection of drums shown here are by Randy Two-Eagles Billings. (See Appendix Four)

The "talking stick," pictured here, was used to speak to the Spirits.

The shaman would strike the earth three times, like knocking on the door. Entering one of the three realms, the shaman would have a spirit guide with him or her. My picture here has a hand- carved blackbird on the top, feathers and beads hanging on a leather thong. I put a rubber cup on its bottom to protect flooring in any homes I visit, or places where I lecture.

In addition to these “tools,” the shaman has a wide variety of herbs and crystals to use in the treatment of a client.

Generally speaking, I am not referencing the garden type variety of plants but those that grow naturally in the wild. Soil and rain have much to do with the value of the plants. Would I use commercial herbs and herbals? Yes, if I could not obtain organics. Today, however, organics have become readily available, if not locally, certainly via the Internet. Be sure to check the source. The issue is chemical fertilizer. Appendix One lists some of the available herbs and their medicinal uses.

V - SMUDGING

Because smudging is such an essential ingredient of healing I feel it deserves a separate chapter. However, before I begin to smudge a client or a room I use a version of a dosing rod. It is a simple construction consisting of a piece of a metal clothes hanger and a piece of a plastic straw. (See illustration) One end is bent and inserted into the two inches of plastic straw. I prefer to use the straw rather than my fingers because it removes any question about the possibility of my moving the piece of wire with my fingers. The rod is used to determine the energy flow of the room and of the client. It if swings to the right the energy is positive, to the left it is negative energy and if it remains stationary, it indicates a lack of energy. These last two provide necessary clues to the healer as to what the client's issues may be.

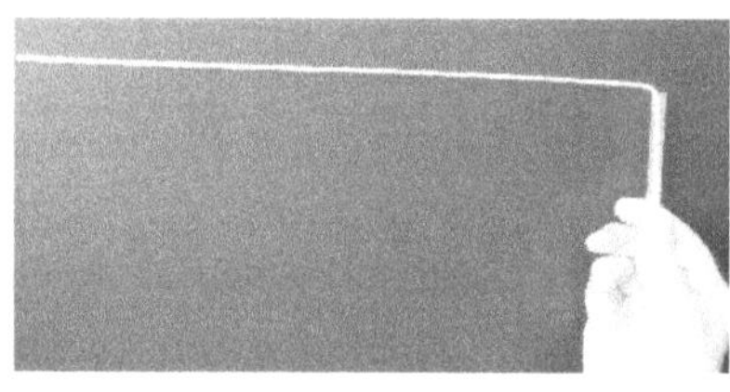

Smudging, a traditional activity among some Native Americans, has entered the venue of controversy. The claim by some Native Americans is that there has been a cultural misappropriation. Terms such as smudge sticks, sage bundles, and smudging kits are an affront to some Native Americans. Please note not all Native Americans or First People of Canada smudge. And for some, "smoke" is used in special sacred ceremonies. As a healer, I use it for purification and or cleansing of the soul, of one's home or other buildings. Its function is to rid the person and the area in which he or she is of negativity and to begin the healing processes. An additional purpose of smudging is to rid an area of a lingering spirit. I was called in by a new owner of a large home with a fantastic ocean view. Because a murder had taken place there the owners felt there was a presence and it was making them uncomfortable. I did a white sage smudge throughout the house, including the three-stall garage and basement. Then I did a complete smudge around the outside of the house. A couple of months later the owners let me know they no longer felt the presence that was making them feel uncomfortable.

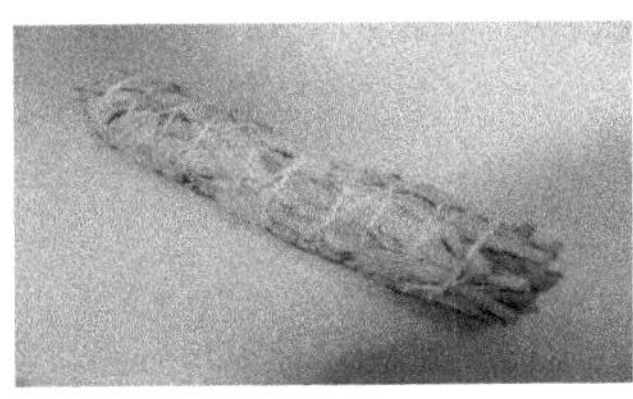

In addition to sage (The bundle shown here is of white sage handpicked in the mountains of California), cedar, palo santo, and or sweetgrass may be added to the mixture in the sea shell. I general add copal to make it burn longer and to sweeten. By the way, if a sea shell is not available any non-breakable small dish may be used.

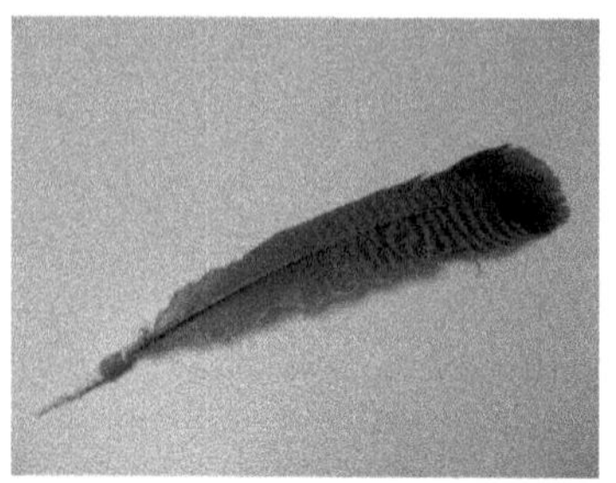

There are four aspects involved in smudging: traditionally the sea shell (represents the element of water), four sacred plants (cedar, sage, sweetgrass, and tobacco represents the element, earth), fire from a match or lighter, represents the third element, and fourth, the smoke produced from lighting the materials in the sea shell, represents air, the fourth element. Once the smudging material is lighted, a turkey feather fan is used to waft the smoke over and around the client. The rest of the room may be smudged. The turkey feather fan pictured was a gift from a Creek, who killed the turkey, then arranged a blessing before presenting it to me. Native Americans are allowed to have Eagle feathers, by Federal law, others are not.

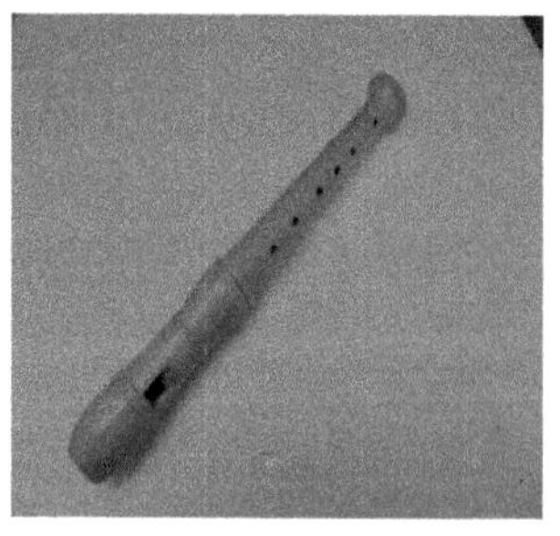

Another instrument used by shaman to create change in a client's vibrational pattern is the wooden flute. Flutes have been around for at least 35,000 years. They have been found in nearly all cultures and every continent in the world. Flutes, depending upon the player, produce a variety of tones, often haunting and ethereal.

Used to appease the gods, to soothe spirits, or to quiet a client, flutes are a mainstay of the shamanic medicine bag. The one pictured here is modern and made of wood.

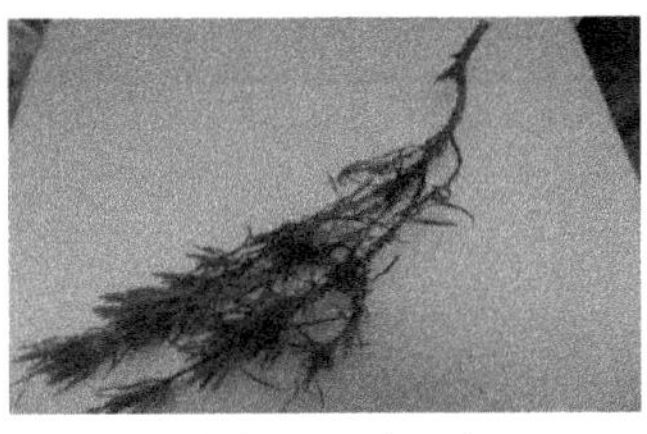

Shaman also use what we now call "essential oils". Unlike modern methods of distillation, the shaman of old, cooked down the plants, removed the plant material from the hot water, and then skimmed off the oil. Lavender, (pictured) for example, was and still is a plant with multiple uses. It's a wonderful disinfectant, excellent for calming, cleansing an area for treatment, and a flavor for foods. Rosemary is another favorite and like lavender, it has many uses. With over 700 plants containing essential oils, the shaman was limited only by his or her skills and by the plants available in his immediate environment. More is said about essential oils in Chapter IX. Appendix Three lists some of the essential oils and their potential uses.

The shaman has one other "tool" in his medicine bag. I have briefly mentioned the shaman going into a hypnotic trance to travel to another realm. Some shaman use hallucinogenic drugs to achieve a trance-like state; others use the drum. The trance processes deserve further discussion as do the purposes of the trance state.

The natural healing from within each of us is the greatest force for getting well.

Hippocrates

VI - THE SHAMANIC TRANCE

I want to begin this section with a quote from the late Michael Harner. In his book, *Cave and Cosmos* (Berkeley. North Atlantic Books, 2013) Harner states, "The drum not only helps one travel shamanically but stimulates visionary experience." (43) Travel and vision are interconnected. Visionary, however, suggests something more than "seeing." Implied is a future orientation. During the trance, the shaman sees what is to be done to help a client. He or she would, in earlier times, receive information regarding a future move of the tribe, or to change hunting grounds.

Travel to another realm of which there are three fascinates people. But experience dictates that one may travel to more than the three realms called Upper, Middle, and Lower. Current thinking in science suggests there are at least ten dimensions, a shock to traditional thinking that has indicated we have only three dimensions. Some suggest twelve dimensions. Rainey Marie Highly has written about a thirteenth dimension.

The drum is the instrument of choice. If you have a friend who can strike a consistent slow beat on a hand-held drum, you can begin your journey. However, if you do not, there are a number of people including Michael Harner, Kenneth Meadow, Sandra Ingerman have commented on drumming and have CDs or Mp3 files available. In 1962 Andrew Neher in "A Psychological Explanation of Unusual Behavior in

Ceremonies Involving Drums" pointed out drumming produces changes in our central nervous system. It affects the electrical activity in several areas of the brain and creates a trance condition.

Melinda C. Maxwell, PhD. has in her "Effects of Rhythmic Drumming on EEG and Subjective Experience" (Dissertation, 1990) laid out a scientific basis for a particular drum beat.

The number recommended beats per second vary. Dr. Maxwell found that a steady rhythmic beat of a drum struck 4 ½ times per second was the key to transporting one into a trance state. Others suggest 120 beats per minute. That's about two beats per second. To bring a shaman back from his or her trance, the drummer increases the beats to at least three beats per second. This normally lasts about two minutes.

A question often asked of me is about how long a trance should last. As a rule of thumb, I recommend no more than fifteen minutes. The drummer, at the end of that time, should begin rapidly drumming. The person in the trance may think it has been much longer or even shorter. The experienced shaman will not question the time frame. I have to urge a caution here. Do not try to make the trance last a long time. The danger is twofold: the purpose of the visit to another realm may be lost and second, there is the potential of irreparable psychological damage to the person in the trance. I urge extreme caution if you are going to try to travel to another realm make sure your drummer is experienced in such things. If you are doing this for the first time, have an experienced traveler with you.

A second question I am often asked is how deep a trance should one have. First and foremost, the depth of a trance depends upon the individual involved. The depth is also determined by the purpose of the trance. A shamanic trance is much different from a "parlor-game" trance, or one that is designed to reduce pain or one that is designed to take a person on a shamanic journey to find a "teacher."

Years ago, to demonstrate this difference, I had a group of my college students [10] place their right hand up in the air while a second group watched. The students with their right hand in the air were taken into a trance. They were then asked to move their right hand. They could not. This condition, by the way, is called *catalepsy.* Next, I took them on a timed "out-of-body" experience. We spent the rest of the class time debriefing the experience. The difference between just a trance and an out-of-body experience became immediately clear. They were not aware of not being able to move their right hand; they were aware of travelling and seeing themselves doing it.

The trance that a shaman goes into is deeper, but not so deep that he or she cannot function. During this trance, one's eyes may flutter, one may even have open "unseeing" eyes. This is not what is referred to as a somnambulistic state. During the trance, the shaman may opt to travel to one of three realms. These are commonly called The Upper Realm, The Middle Realm, and the Lower Realm. Do not confuse these or equate these with religious concepts of Heaven, Purgatory, and Hell. They are entirely different. Punishments and rewards are not associated with the shamanic realms. However, do not misconstrue this to mean members of the Spirit World will not extract just due if they are so inclined.

Finally, do not attempt to travel to another realm as a means of entertainment. You will be rebuffed. One should only go to another real to seek information, to get help, or to get guidance.

VII - THE REALMS

As with any journey to the world of the Spirits, one does not go for a vacation or a grand tour. The Universe does not like generalities and neither does the Spirit World. It is absolutely essential that one goes with respect. The stories from the ancient world contain many examples of people who entered the Spirit World in a disrespectful way and were not allowed to leave. Disrespectful also means not following established protocol to the letter.

The Upper realm basically houses teachers and ascended ones, and souls of deceased humans. Spirits who live in this realm are considered safe to interact with and their energy is directly connected to the ultimate energy, the Source.

Some people are now including angels and archangels brought in from various religions. These did not exist for the early shaman. Frankly, I am not sure the shaman of old made any distinctions other than broad general ones such as speaking to an "ascended one."

The shaman, while in a deep trance, travels to the Upper Realm to seek advice from those who abide there. He or she goes with a specific question. More often than not, the shaman will be given an answer to his quest. The shaman, for example, may be directed to use "sucking" on his client. More about that later.

The Middle Realm contains human spirits and souls that have not been released. By this, I mean those entities that are earthbound Spirits and those souls that have not crossed over. This realm exists just outside of the reality in which we presently live. It is from here that we meet ghosts, sometimes the souls of our loved ones and that includes our pets. The shaman would travel to this realm because a recent relative or an ancestor would have insights into the client's illness or needs.

The Lower Realm is in the earth and it is primarily the realm of nature spirits, animal spirits, and what is commonly called "lost" souls. Sometimes the spirits that inhabit this realm are not always cooperative. I don't want to use the word evil to describe their behavior because it would not be true, but they sometimes are not very nice. A trip to this realm by a shaman would be to find out what herbs and plants he or she should use in the treatment of a client.

Previously I mentioned that some scientists are claiming there are as many as ten dimensions while others say there are twelve. I have written about the twelfth dimension. (September 2013, EzineArticles.com) Some writers about shamanic journeying now include these dimensions as sub divisions of the three standard realms. My experience suggests there certainly is something similar to that.

A number of years ago, a young woman in my philosophy class missed a good deal of the semester because she was involved in a tragic automobile accident in which her fiancé was killed. She spent several weeks hospitalized because of her own injuries. She stopped by my office and asked if I would take her on a journey. She wanted to know how she got under her fiancé's body. The police had told her that was where they found her. Using a CD with drumming on it, I put her into a trance. I heard her say, "Oh no!" and she began to sob. I spoke her name to bring her out of the trance. When I asked her to tell me about her experience she told me she saw the accident and that her fiancé had thrown himself over her, thus saving her life at the cost of his own. A large shard of glass had penetrated his back and severed an artery to his heart. She had suffered several fractures and internal injuries. Sometime later while I was crossing the campus she saw me and flagged me down. She told me she finally was at peace because she knew what happened.

For me, this suggests there is a place and a time when past events can be seen because they are still happening. And if that's true, then it must be equally true that under certain conditions, one can see the future before it happens and change it. It's a wonderful lesson and reminder that the spiritual world overlaps the physical world. Both need our respect.

Speaking of respect, one thing I wish to emphasize is to always thank the Spirit World as you leave. This applies to the shaman as well as the client if he or she is traveling.

There are four general reasons for visiting another realm. The most common reason is to seek help for the client. The shaman travels to retrieve a lost or stolen soul, or a part of a soul. The third reason a shaman visits one of the realms is to get a reading for future events, and finally, the shaman travels to get help in assuring the success of a particular endeavor.

VIII - PROTOCOL

I have spoken of the necessity to follow protocol when engaged with Spirits and the Spirit World. Disrespect can bring irrevocable physical and psychological harm. I cannot emphasize this enough.

A fair question is how does one know what behavior to follow when approaching the Spirit World. Tradition sets the standard. I am well aware of the contemporary mantra that tradition needs to be changed to comply with the modern world. However modern one is, it does not excuse rudeness or bad behavior.

Traditionally, a shaman will spend time in what we now call meditation before he begins a journey to another realm. After this quiet time, a prayer is offered. The shaman will offer a prayer to each of the four directions. Some may add two or three additional directions depending on the tribal affiliation. The seven directions are East, South, West, North, Above, Center, Below.

Prayers differ from tribe to tribe. The shaman may offer the "pipe" to each of the directions. The pipe and tobacco play a significant role in many ceremonies. The pipes vary in size. Their bowls are generally made of local clay or are carved out of wood. The tobacco is a mixture consisting of red willow or red osier dogwood, Kinnickinnick, and other native plants.

I offer white sage or Palo Santo to each of the four directions. I pause at each direction. It would be disrespectful to zip through the process. I keep my prayer relatively short and simple. [11] Following is one example.

Spirit of the East
Where the eye of the Sun wakens
Spirit of the South
Where warmth bathes us
Spirit of the West
Where the Sun closes its eye
Spirit of the North
Where the wind blows the truth,
Grant my request.

I want to digress for a moment because my short prayer offers a good example. When you go to the Spirit World or the Universe don't plead, beg, or crawl while seeking help. You must command. This does not mean being rude or obnoxious. Notice the last line of my prayer. "Grant my request" is a command. It's a declarative statement with the subject (you) understood.

When I am doing a healing I use the same prayer, not spoken aloud, and add "to bring healing energy to (client's first name)."

I slowly move in a circle, going from one of the four directions to another. My body completes the spiral and acts as a conduit for Universal energy to flow downward. The spiral which appears in all of nature is a power source and one that holds great promise.

IX - INTENTION

Earlier I used the word intention. I want to come back to that because its understanding and its role in healing is so very significant. What does intention mean? According to Dictionary.com, an intention is "an act or instance of determining mentally upon some action or result." Put another way, an intention is deciding you want something or are going to do something. Certainly sounds simple enough, doesn't it?

In the initial client interview, it is paramount that the client's intention is clearly stated, the implications and ramifications are understood by the client, and the intention is morally sound. By morally sound, I am not establishing a religious covenant, but I am making sure the intention by the client is not to harm another human being. A woman who was having serious marital problems asked me to do something to her husband. I do not, let me repeat that, I do not place curses, hexes, or any other harmful activity on anyone. That defeats the purpose of being a healer.

Failure is almost guaranteed if the intention is not specific based. An example of a non-specific based intention is "I want to be well." A specifically based intention is "I want to stop having headaches." This can be made even more specific: "I want to stop having headaches when I wake up in the morning." This can be even more specific: "I want to stop having frontal headaches when I wake up in the morning."

A technique I recommend to help the client concentrate on his or her intention is to have that individual do two things; first, to write down the intention and second to say it out loud, three times. I urge the client to repeat the intention each morning just before getting out of bed. This is a subtle way of reinforcing and strengthening the intention. I prefer having the client repeat the intention in the morning before getting out of bed because saying it at night may flip the intention to a concentration on the person's illness and thus cause a restless or sleepless night. Specific intention is crucial. When I lecture on manifesting I stress the importance of proper intention setting. I mention manifesting because sometimes that is what a client needs to know how to do. One can manifest improved health. Again this is something that would be determined and decided upon during the initial client interview.

X - THE JOURNEY

Often I am asked: What is a shamanic journey like. What happens? What do you see? Where do you go? Answers will vary as do people who journey. For me, it is not always easy to put into words. My first journey as an adult took place at The Lac à l'Eau Claire, Quebec, Canada. It was the last trip I made into Canada with my father. He and a family friend had decided it was good for me since I had been having some health issues, specifically a sticky heart valve. That year the snow was still on the ground and much of the lake was still frozen. "Good for ice fishing," my father had said.

I did not complete my last semester of college, but because I had enough credits to graduate I came back in late June for graduation.

The front of the three-bedroom cabin was all glass, offering up a panoramic view of Clear Lake. In front of the windows were two large leather recliners with wooden side arms. I was sitting in one of those staring out at the bright blue sky. My father and his friend, John had gone into town to get supplies. Actually, I think they went into town to get liquored-up.

I began to deep breathe, slowly at first, and then gradually increased the number of breaths per minute. I did not have a drum. Rapid deep breathing works just fine. The caution here is not to hyperventilate. Shortly after closing my eyes, a blue orb appeared. Suddenly, it liquefied and everything became a mass of the most beautiful deep dark indigo I had ever seen. The swirling mass picked me up. I swear I felt the wind on my cheeks. Just as suddenly, the swirling mass of indigo stopped and I stopped, suspended in time. A dark-skinned man's face appeared. A mass of long braided white hair tumbled down around his weathered face. There was no body. He pursed his lips and blew at me. I felt a slight breeze on my face. It was then I recognized who it was, Esaugetuh, the Master of Breath. He nodded at me and disappeared. As the day wore on I began to feel immensely better.

Little did I know at that time, he would be my spirit guide and would be the name I called when using my obsidian pendulum to channel the Spirit World.

XI - CRYSTALS AND HEALING

What are crystals? Much is being written about crystals and many businesses revolve around the sale of crystals.

At Dictionary.com a crystal is defined as, "A material in which the atoms are arranged in a rigid geometrical structure marked by symmetry. Crystals often have clearly visible geometrical shapes." Kinds of crystals, color, and type, as well as their geometrical structure, play a significant role in determining their use and value.

I began my studies of crystals with a wonderful and informative teacher, Anna Sundari Knight. During my two classes with her, I learned that crystals have specific purposes such as recorder, transformer, and communicator. Those two classes were just enough to encourage further investigation. As a result of that investigation, I was invited to be a member of the Crystal Vaults Inner Circle and after an intensive program, I was certified as a Crystal Practitioner.

How do crystals heal? Each crystal has its own unique vibration that impacts the physical and emotional levels of the individual, which allows healing to occur.

There is archaeological evidence that Native Americans used crystals at least 10,000 years ago. Sites have been revealed in California that supports that contention. Two singular aspects of crystals make them unique: they are of the earth and of the sky. Consequently, their healing power comes from two strong sources.

I will relate just one story about the use of crystals. My niece and her nurse friend were visiting my home. I decided I'd do the man thing and cook steaks on the grill. Once they were cooked to order, I removed them to a warm platter, reached up to close the grill lid. I missed and put my hand on the still lit grill that had been heating at 450 degrees. I managed to get back into the house, sat the steaks down, grabbed a clear quartz crystal and held it in my burnt hand. Within a couple of minutes, the pain was gone, no blisters showed up, and of course, no scaring.

Clear quartz is a wonderful healing crystal not only for physical issues by emotional ones as well. Another popular crystal is amethyst. It is a strong healer as well as protector. Often, people look for their power crystal, one that is especially tuned to them. My power crystal is obsidian, shown here. It is carved into the shape of an arrow head, wrapped in silver. I use it as a pendulum when I wish to access the spirit world without going into a trance. The pouch to its right is to carry it in.

One that I keep at my desk is black tourmaline and clear quartz in what is called a Pyramid Extractor. It is a powerful tool for bringing immediate relief of pain. I use it for cranky fingers, headache, and neck pain caused by long hours at the computer. The clear quartz is shaped like a pyramid, with the black tourmaline attached as four prongs. (see photo) I sometimes place this on a person who complains of a particular pain in a leg, arm, hip, neck, or a headache to give them near immediate relief. To "suck" the pain way, I place the point of the pyramid on the impacted area. To heal, I place the flat side of the pyramid on the area.

Crystals have a long and varied use. Crystals can and do neutralize negativity, clear blockages created by trauma, and help restore a sense of harmony. They can be carried around with you, placed in your automobile, in your office, under your pillow, or on a nightstand. Crystals are used to create jewelry. That does not diminish their effectiveness.

XII - ESSENTIAL OILS AND HEALING

An essential oil is simply a concentrated hydrophobic liquid. This liquid contains high aroma compounds and can be made from a wide variety of plants. Because of a very distinctive scent, or essence, the names used to identify them include volatile oils, ethereal oils, and aethorolea or more commonly, essential oils. There are several ways by which essences of plant oils are abstracted. Among these are steam distillation, Co2, absolutes, and cold pressing. Steam distillation is the most common method of abstraction used.

Just to provide emphasis on the value of essential oils please note that it takes 2,000 pounds of rose petals to make 16 ounces of essential rose oil. It takes 50 pounds of Eucalyptus leaves, 150 pounds of Lavender flowers, 500 hundred pounds of Rosemary plants, and 1,000 pounds of jasmine flowers to create their essential oils. You now have a reason why pure essential oils are so expensive.

Keep in mind that not all essential oils are *pure oils* and therein lies the rub. Not all essential oils are the same. Furthermore, one doesn't just dab on a pure essential oil. It would be over-powering and may cause severe reactions. Generally, the essential oil is mixed with jojoba oil. Make sure you check the source of your essential oils. Remember the old adage "you get what you pay for" holds true for essential oils.

Essential oils have a direct correlation to vibration. They start at 52Hz and go as high as 320 Hz, which is the frequency of rose oil. Therapeutic grade essential oils have the highest frequency of any natural substance known to mankind; thus creating a bacteria, fungus, and virus free environment. That is one large reason for making sure you get quality essential oils.

No matter the essential oil, it has a vibrational frequency as does your body. Low frequencies soak up negative energy and make physical changes in your body. Middle frequencies make emotional changes and high frequencies make spiritual changes and these range from 92 Hz to 360 Hz.

The shaman may not know the vibrational frequencies of an essential oil, but she or he knows which oils work. My essential oils teacher, Susanna Mantis, claims it takes only 20 seconds for an essential oil when applied to the skin, to enter the blood stream. That's powerful! Appendix Three lists some of the many uses of essential oils and which oil to use with which issue.

XIII - VIBRATION

Albert Einstein has said, "everything in life is vibration." And so it is. And when that vibration is out of sync not only does the universe and the earth respond, so does the human body. Ancient shaman understood this. In Chapter IV I mentioned the tools used to change the vibrational patterns of a client. Modern healers talk about blockages. Blockages and out of sync vibrations are the same things.

Some fundamental science information will provide ample proof of the Einstein statement quoted above. As I wrote in *Shamanic Manifesting* (Published 2015) there are 327.2 trillion cells in the human body. We are told there are 100 trillion atoms in just one cell. The number of atoms in the human body is seven octillion. Our solar system has three hundred three quindecillion, three hundred fifty five quattuordecillion atoms (that's 45 zeros) and all of these are vibrating. Synchronization is essential. When that synchronization falters we become cranky, angry, depressed, and or ill.

Every cell in your body is vibrating constantly. This vibration can be directed and enhanced through the power of sound frequencies in the form of words and the beat of a drum, or in today's world, created sound waves that resonate at specific MHz, something the late Bruce Tainio of Tainio Technologies identified for the human body. The healthy human body has a frequency of 62-72 Hz. The human brain's frequency is 72-80 MHz.

Even though some of this seems off the wall, it is not and it is by no means new. Ancient Rishis, Seers, and Yogis of India developed mantras that play upon the effectiveness of sound for enhancing consciousness and inducing healing of the mind and body. Sports injuries are now healed by using sound. Mothers have always sung to their newborn babies. Babies make repetitive sounds over and over again. Both are to induce quietness, calm and sleep.

For those of you who are interested in Solfeggio here are the Solfeggio Frequencies and the areas they help improve.

UT – 396 Hz – Liberating Guilt and Fear
RE – 417 Hz – Undoing Situations and Facilitating Change
MI – 528 Hz – Transformation and DNA Repair
FA – 639 Hz – Connecting/Relationships
SOL – 741 Hz – Awakening Intuition
LA – 852 Hz – Returning to Spiritual Order

The Marconi Union in collaboration with sound therapist created and recorded *Weightless*. According to reports, listening to the harmonics lead to a 65% reduction in the anxiety of the participants in a study. Jonathan Goldman's recording *The Divine Name I Am* based on the ancient Gregorian Chants is another excellent use of Hz.

XIV - THE HEALING: BACKGROUND

There are purists in the integrated healing professions. As with anything, one has to buy into the program and then it becomes one's own. Subtle changes creep in. I have watched other Reiki healers, ARC healers, and Shamanic Healers. I am sure my own practice differs and that is not to mean I feel or believe mine is superior. My approach has been somewhat modified since my certification as a spiritual counselor.

From now on I will refer to the client rather than to the client. I meet with the client to determine what their expectations are. What is it they want from a healing. During that aspect of our meeting, I ask about the nature of an illness, medical treatment, and drugs being taken. The conversation will vary if the client indicates emotional issues. I do not play psychologist.

A part of my initial interview process is to determine if we will be a good fit. Then I try to determine the client's commitment to getting help and following through with treatment. I give them a three-part assignment which requires a phone call from the client back to me. An email is also acceptable. One example of the three-part assignment will suffice. If the client has "them" issues I ask that he or she list five things they like about themselves. If the client issue is physical, I ask them if they would like a "distance healing" and arrange for them to be at home and up at 6 AM. I will call them and if they do not answer the phone on the first ring I question their intention. Sometimes I deliberately do not call. If I get a phone call or an email message from the client checking to see why I hadn't called I have a strong indication of the person making a commitment.

I mentioned the word intention. Client intention is extremely important. It is essential if any healing is to take place. On the surface, this sounds easy enough but what is demanded is a belief that the individual can heal her or himself. One's belief system always plays an integral part of healing and this holds true in medicine and psychiatry as well as integrative healing procedures.

I also have the client do a check sheet in which he or she indicates allergies to herbs and ingredients in essential oils and noting any known medical conditions.

would conclude my first session with a client. I most likely do something that other healers may not do. I do not charge for the initial meeting. If the client and I feel comfortable I will then determine the number of sessions that would be appropriate. Generally, I schedule only two and then with the client make a determination if further appointments are necessary. This allows both of us to evaluate progress. At this point, I can get a feeling about the client's attitude.

Another purpose of setting two sessions is to allay the potentiality of a client "fixating" on me by engaging more sessions than necessary. I also have a concern that less than ethical practitioners all too often require more “healing” sessions than may be necessary.

XV - THE HEALING: SETTING

Since I do not maintain an office I carry with me certain items that create an *altar*. This is done for a couple of reasons: First, it sets the tone for the healing session and second, it brings the power of crystals into the healing area. Altars, like techniques used, vary. Those in physical offices are sometimes quite elaborate. This is not a criticism. Each healer has the right to express themselves in any way they wish. Some do not use altars because it may suggest a religious overtone.

My altar contains a small statue of Buddha, a carved eagle sitting on a white quartz mountain, moldavite, clear quartz crystal, selenite obelisk, fluorite obelisk, and tangerine sun aura quartz. These are the staple group. Occasionally, other crystals are added depending upon the perceived need of the client. What is the purpose of each of my altar items?

The Buddha is to remind me of the sanctity of ancient wisdom. The eagle is my spirit guide and protector. The moldavite, often considered the most powerful crystal on earth and one of the rarest is to remind me that we are all made of star stuff. The clear quartz crystal and the selenite obelisk are great healers. The fluorite obelisk is a generator crystal. A generator crystal is superior for energy magnification, generation, and focus. It is used to promote an energized environment and it helps break through complex problems. The final piece on my altar is tangerine sun aura quartz and is noted for its dynamic energy and is a wonderful crystal for dispensing dark moods.

As you see, my altar is aimed at the generation of energy. Energy heals. Energy is vibration and in keeping with my healing mission, the preponderance of positive vibration is essential for a change in both physical and emotional health and well-being of any client. I do not discuss my altar or even mention it. If the client asks, I say it's for generating positive energy.

XVI - THE HEALING: PROCEDURES

Be aware that the following described procedures may not be what another healer would use or they may add other procedures such as calling upon some of the Archangels.

After making sure the client is comfortable, I use a mixture of sage, Palo Santo, and cedar placed in a small dish and set on fire to smudge the room and then the client. The client may be seated or may be lying on a massage table. The client is asked to keep his or her clothes on, expect for shoes and socks. A warmed, soft blanket covers the client. With pre-session approval, I rub a small amount of an essential oil into each foot. I then wrap both feet in a warm towel. I use an essential oil specially blended for me. I generally use pure Palo Santo oil mixed with rosemary and jojoba as the emulsifier. After that, I wash my hands if a sink is conveniently located. If not, I carry a small bottle of lavender hydrosol and use that to clean my hands.

The warm blanket, essential oil, and warm towel helps the comfort level of the client and continues the cleansing of negative energy. If the client has indicated a particular issue, I may smudge again. I will take the smudging fan in a downward and out sweeping movement from the head to the feet.

After the smudging, I give my client a crystal to hold during the healing session. Depending on the need, I generally choose amethyst, an all-around healer. I will also place specific crystals around the client. If he or she is seated, I will place them around the person's chair. If the client is laying down, I will place crystals at various points along his or her body.

To continue the relaxation of the client, I take him or her through a five-minute breathing exercise. At the end of which I start a CD of drumming. Michael Harner and Kenneth Mathews have excellent drumming CDs available. (See bibliography for a listing of CD's as well as books.) This is to take the client into a controlled semi-hypnotic state. The volume of the drumming is kept just at an audible level as background. From my perspective, this enhances the healing hand's movements I use during a session.

I begin at the client's shoulders. (I have asked if there is any issue if I physically touch the client. If there is, I keep my hands a few inches above the individual's body.) Some healers, believing the feet are the first source of "earth energy," begin with the feet. The client may feel warmth, cool, or a light vibration coming from my hands. Some may feel nothing. I explain this to the client prior to the beginning of the healing session.

It is important that the client understands that he or she may not feel or sense an immediate change in their being. It may take a couple of days. The change may be subtle, even something simple as the client suddenly humming.

Sometimes, depending on the direction I receive from my Spirit Guide, I will take my first two fingers of each hand, hold them together, tuck the remaining two under my thumb. I will place the two extended fingers at the far end of each shoulder of the client. I will leave them there for a couple of minutes. Next, I flatten my hands and pass them over each shoulder, allowing them to come to rest on the shoulders. I tell the client that my hands will be resting on their shoulders.

Next, I place both hands on the back of the client's neck. I prefer to have my two middle fingers barely touch one another. For me, this completes the circle of energy, allowing it to flow continuously. Then I move so the client's head is cradled in my hands and I gently move my fingers in a circular motion, slowly working my way to the top of the head. I also very gently tap all around the scalp. Again, this is to increase energy flow. (Tapping or EFT healing, as it is technically called blends in very nicely.)

I slowly move my hands down the rest of the client's body. Because of my sensitivity to women and men's right to respect and privacy, I do not touch their private parts. I raise my hands a couple of inches above those areas. My client's physical privacy is a top priority along with a commitment to his or her confidentiality.

A couple of comments about confidentiality is appropriate at this juncture. Because I am a certified spiritual counselor and operate under that banner, my client and I are both legally protected. The bond is as strong as attorney-client confidentiality, or communicant and priest.

Once I have reached the person's feet, I begin working my way back up the client's body. Sometimes my hands will linger over a particular spot. To me, this is an indication of an energy blockage. Once the healing session is done, I suggest the client checks with his or her medical doctor and discuss that blocked area. I take considerable time to explain to the client that my lingering over a particular part of his or her body does not necessarily indicate something is seriously wrong. I am a strong advocate of checking with one's medical doctor. Their knowledge base and science differ from mine. We have the same goal but with different approaches. The old saying "don't throw out the baby with the bath water" holds true. Don't cross out your family doctor.

Once I have completed the healing, I lean over and speak into the client's ear and say, "Nepilatl." This is a Mi'kmaq word that means "heal." To the best of my ability, I think it is pronounced *neh pee la tu.* It belongs to the same word family that Say-pie used to call me "Healer." (Notice that I simply said the word as a command.)

There is a very old healing technique, which I mentioned earlier and one I do not use. It is called "sucking." The shaman leans over the person and moves from the top of the head to the feet making sucking and spitting noises. The implication is that the healer is sucking out the sickness or evil spirits from the person. When I have had Reiki healing treatments I have noticed a spitting sound by the healer.

XVII - HEALING YOURSELF: THE SHAMAN'S WAY

It holds true that in all healing modalities, there are certain things you may do to help self-healing. The following exercises are designed to help you restore your physical and emotional energy, thus, helping you to heal yourself. As with, all self-improvement practices always listen to what your body tells you. If something doesn't feel right, stop doing it.

Not everyone will immediately feel energized nor will they feel an immediate improvement. That may take a couple of days or longer. The practice may need to be repeated on a daily basis for a week or two before you sense and feel a positive change.

The first thing you should do is check your current energy level. The following three exercises are designed to do that. You may want to do more than one as a way to cross check your energy reading.

EXERCISES TO ASSESS YOUR ENERGY

Exercise One

A simple, yet effective thing to do, is to rub your hands together in a circular motion. Generally, healers do not have a preference, however, I do. Place the palms together and rub them together so that your dominate hand comes back to your heart. I feel this brings Universal energy to your body rather than taking energy from your body and sending it out into the Universe. The heart is a wonderfully fantastic producer of energy.

rubbing the palms of your hands together for two to three minutes, separate the palms, keeping them facing one another. Gently push your dominate hand back and forth from the non-dominate hand. In my case, I keep my left hand still and move my right hand in and out. Make sure your hands to not touch one another. You should feel a slight pressure on the palms of your hands. You may also sense or feel a mild warmth.

If you feel neither pressure or warmth, you are getting a reasonable indication that you need to give your energy level a boost.

Exercise Two

This exercise may baffle you and much of its success depends upon your attitude. Like Exercise One, it is simple and can be done wherever you are, except if you are driving an automobile.

Raise your arms, elbows close to each side of your chest, hands with palms facing outward, and slightly cupped. Wait two to three minutes and then turn your cupped hands inward to your face, as if you were splashing water on your face.

Your hands act as antennae, and you are bringing energy to your upper chakras. You should feel a slightly warmed air on your face. If you do not, this is another indication your energy level is low.

Exercise Three

Slowly rub your hands together. Gradually increase the speed of your rubbing. Total time about one minute. Place both hands in front of your eyes, palms facing your face. Gradually, move your hands to the top of your head, the crown chakra.

You should feel a warmth or slight vibration from your hands. If you do not, then you have an indicator that you need to boost your energy level.

EXERCISES FOR SELF-RESTORATION OF ENERGY

Restoring energy does require patience and a core belief that energy can be restored. Certain drugs can pep you up and they can be addictive. What is offered here is a different choice and hopefully one with a longer lasting benefit. A lack of result or progress may mean you need professional assistance.

Exercise One

I have said your core belief system is important to your energy and the generation of energy. Try the following: Say the following sentence over and over again for 20 or 30 seconds: *The world is full of violence*. Notice how you feel. Now say the following sentence over and over again for 20 or 30 seconds: *The world is filled with love*. Again notice how you feel.

Probably you lost that earlier negativity created by the first sentence. Your belief system which encompasses your attitude can generate positive or negative energy. A variation on this is to make it personal: *My world is full of (you put in your word here)* and then switch it to My *world is filled with love*. Notice how you feel.

Exercise Two

Sit in a comfortable position. Close your eyes. Take three deep breaths. Hold your breath each time to the count of three before exhaling. Now think the color orange. Once the color is clear, think of an orange ball floating above your head. Tilt your head back, open your mouth, and let the orange ball fill you with warm energy. Hold this pose for a couple of minutes. Do not strain or put uncomfortable pressure on your neck. *Hint:* Try this just after you get out of bed in the morning.

Exercise Three

This exercise has two versions. Both are designed to bring positive energy to you.

The first version: Bring the first two fingers (Index and Middle) of each hand together as you would if pointing at something. Your thumbs are to cover your other two fingers. (Ring and baby finger) With the first two fingers, lightly press them to your temples. Just hold them there for a couple of minutes. Next, gently rub your temples in a clockwise circle. Do that for a couple of minutes. You should have a warm feeling.

Using this same finger configuration is a good way to bring energy to an aching muscle. Additionally, if you have ever experience forgetting a person's name, the name of a book, or a street name, or a lost thought place the index and middle fingers, held together, on one of your temples, close your eyes. The lost name will come to you.

The second version is somewhat more complicated and requires some additional moves. As directed above bring the index and middle fingers together. The ring finger and littler finger should form a circle when positioned with the thumb. Do this with both hands.

If you ever created a shadow figure of a rabbit's head, you used this configuration. Next, using your dominate hand, draw a circle in front of you, a few inches from your body. Now insert the two fingers of the dominate hand into the circle formed by the ring finger, little finger, and thumb of the other hand. Turn your hands so they face you, open the fingers of the non-dominate hand. You will have three fingers facing you. You are releasing Universal energy into your body.

You may have the open fingers face your third eye chakra or your heart chakra. I prefer the heart chakra because the heart is the center of much energy and does so much more than pump blood.

A reminder: As with all of these exercises the shift in energy or the feeling of energy flowing will be subtle. Just because you do not immediately feel something doesn't mean that nothing is happening.

Exercise Four

Literature and healing practitioners often speak of "blockages," something that is preventing the normal flow of energy to various body parts. It is also used to refer to psychological issues that clients may be experiencing. This exercise, like the others presented here, is simple and does not consume a lot of your time. Its purpose is to move the energy either through a blockage or around it so you feel better.

You may do this exercise seated or standing. Since we are told we do not stand enough, I recommend standing.

Reach both arms above your head, place the palms of your hands together in "prayer pose." Stretch your arms up as far as you comfortably can. Hold that pose for a couple of minutes. Then keeping your hands together, lean to your right. Only go as far as you are comfortable. If you are standing, be aware of any balance issues you may have. Hold that pose for a couple of minutes. Next, slowly straighten up and then bend to your left. Stay there for a couple of minutes and then slowly return to the upright position, lower your arms, shake your hands. Give yourself a minute before you move to another activity.

This exercise is an excellent one to do just after you get up in the morning and it is a great refresher at midday.

Exercise Five

I call this the tent exercise. Raise your arms a couple of inches above your head, place your hands together, palms facing each other. Lower your arms slightly so they make a tent over your head. Image your arms creating a tent that comes down over your body and it contains warm, vibrating energy. Perhaps more like a gentle shower is a better description. Once you feel something, lower your dominate hand to your heart chakra, letting it rest there. Tune into what you feel. Bring your other arm to rest on your abdomen. This should last about two minutes.

You can maintain the pose longer than I have suggested and do so with any of the exercises. I have set a time to minimize your time involvement and any potential physical discomfort. Experiment to determine your own time-comfort zone.

Exercise Six

If you have been on the go all day and at its end, you find yourself tired this exercise will help restore your basic energy. This works best if you are seated in a comfortable chair. Lean forward a little and place a hand on each knee. Do this for about ten minutes.

You will feel refreshed. This is also a good time to do some other self-energy healing exercises.

Exercise Seven

This exercise is a good one if you are feeling cranky, aggressive, or cantankerous. Rub your hands together for a few minutes. Then place your palms over your eyes, making sure hands touch. (The sides of your little fingers should touch.) Take a deep breath, sigh, and just let the warmth of your hands sooth you. Before removing your hands take a couple of deep breaths, holding each for the count of three.

Exercise Eight

Past experience indicates that people have trouble with this exercise. The basic reason is a lack of practice. You most likely will have to practice this daily for a week or more. It is easy to become discouraged because you feel nothing and are distracted with other things. This exercise which I call *creating an energy ball* is a powerful tool in replenishing your physical energy.

Vigorously rub your hands together in a circular motion with your dominate hand moving toward your heart. Do this for at least two minutes. Next, clasp your hands together, making sure the bottom allows no light into your cupped hands, move your thumbs apart just enough so you can see into the center of your hand. Hold your hands up to one eye, closing the other eye. You will see an orange/yellow/red ball. Once you do, toss the ball up into the air, so that it comes down on the top of your head. You will feel an energy renewal.

A side note that may be of interest to you is the energy ball can be programmed. What is meant by that is to set your intention before generating the energy. Make sure your intention (what it is you want) is very clear. You can program your energy ball to do just about anything you want in terms of where you want it to go; chest, heart, spine, head, etc.

For those of you who may be into one or more healing modalities, you can send an energy ball a long distance. Be sure you clearly state to whom and where you want it to go and for what purpose.

At the risk of creating a parlor game, try this: Create your energy ball and then send it to someone in the same room you are in. Your intention is to get them to look at you. The only reason I am giving this tidbit of information is to show you it works.

Practice makes perfect definitely applies to this exercise. Remember, the focus is self-healing.

Exercise Nine

There are times when everyone feels grouchy. Generally speaking, this is caused by negative energy. It has an impact on your personal health and on the emotional stability of everyone around you. There is ample research showing negativity causes stress and sickness. You can clear this negative energy yourself.

Cleanse the area where you are by smudging sage or Palo Santo. You may even want to do this in every room of your house if you are at home. If you are in an office be aware of the impact this might have on others. By the way, Palo Santo comes in a spray mist and that could be used in an office situation.

Once the area has been cleansed, take three deep breaths, counting to three between each. Play a quieting instrumental music piece or one of the available MP3 files with healing sounds. Turn on a single candle. I recommend the battery type candle that flickers rather than a wax candle. There is always a danger the "real" candle could be knocked over and set something on fire. Stare at the candle for a few minutes. Take three more deep breaths. Quietly repeat to yourself several times, "For today I will not be negative." Or say, "I now clear away everything negative."

One time during a session I suggested the "For today I will not be negative" and was immediately chastised for using a negative statement. The person offered this sentence, "For today, I will be positive." If that works for you, do it.

I know some healers suggest jotting down what you feel is causing your negativity. I do not recommend doing that because writing something down reinforces it. It places that which bothers you in front of you as a constant reminder. If writing something down helps you, write something very positive; for example, "I am happy," or "I feel fine."

RELIEVING PHYSICAL PAIN

Chronic pain soon wears down the whole body—both the physical body and the emotional body. One's general health deteriorates as well as does one's personality. Unfortunately, we have become a society composed of "pill poppers." Opiates and their overuse man the national attention. Fortunately, there are things you can do to help relieve your pain that does not require those damaging chemical drugs.

Exercise One

This is for small areas of the body that hurts. Suppose your thumb hurts. Take your index finger of the opposite hand, and gently(GENTLY) stroke the area that hurts. If the wrist area hurts, use the index finger and gently make circular motions on the area that hurts. If the fingers hurt, do the single stroke back and forth on each finger. Do this for five to ten minutes. You have to be the judge of your comfort zone in terms of the amount of time. You can do this on your feet and around your knees. You are not tapping; you are stroking.

Exercise Two

If you are one of those unfortunate people who must stand on cement floors all day and your feet really hurt this exercise is for you. Take two smooth rocks, about the size of a small egg, heat both in hot water. Be sure the stones are not so hot that you can handle them. Hold them on each side of the bottom of your foot. DO NOT heat the stones in a microwave.

Exercise Three

Follow the directions above. This time, however, rub the bottoms of your feet with Rosemary essential oil before applying the heated rocks.

Exercise Four

This exercise was given to me by my Reflexologist. Cover the bottom of a rectangular pan with pebbles. Fill the pan with really warm water, leaving enough room for you to place both feet without spilling the water onto the floor. Add a dozen drops of Rosemary essential oil. Soak your feet until the water cools. Good idea to have a towel handy to dry your feet when you are done.

Exercise Five

Follow the directions given in Exercise Four. Once done, rub both feet with Arnica and then wrap each foot in a warm towel or put warmed socks on your feet.

Exercise Six

This is a quick energizer and pumps oxygen into the lungs and body. Stand up, stretch your arms above your head. Go slowly. Deep breathe for 30 seconds. Lower your arms. Do this two more times.

Exercise Seven

This one is a bit tricky so be careful. If you are not secure in your balance stand next to a wall. In your bare feet, stand up on your toes, come back down. It's a rolling motion. This aids circulation and oxygen flow in the body.

An Invocation to the Seven Directions

We offer our intentions to the East, where the sun rises,

To the South where Springtime begins,

To the West, where autumn reigns,

To the North, where winter commands.

Lift up your faces toward the sky with its many mysteries,

Look to our Mother Earth and offer our intention of gratitude,

Turn now to the center of the group-focus on the red dot-the symbol of our life force-asking that hearts guide our journey.

Unknown author

XVIII - DEALING WITH NEGATIVITY- THE SHAMAN'S WAY

A number of years ago while I was lecturing on the topic love, one of my college students, a Vietnam veteran, stood up and let loose a barrage on what it was like to kill another human being. The proverbial statement, "the room was blue" would be a highly inadequate description. Normally, I would have told him to get out and would have had him removed from my class. Something kicked in and whatever it was, I remained totally calm and looking directly at him said, "I'm glad you feel better." He sat back down in his chair, looking at me with a sheepish half grin. I nodded, continued my lecture. After class, he apologized. What would have been accomplished by threatening him with expulsion from my course or from the campus?

Sometimes negativity builds to a boiling point, other times it is subtle, just under the surface, seething. Both are equally disturbing. Then there are those days when you wake up and just feel crappy. Nothing is right. The coffee is bitter, the eggs are overly cooked, the kids are bickering, the dog wants out, and your spouse is mad because you didn't say good morning. The whole room drips with negativity. What good would be accomplished if you kicked the dog, screamed at the kids, and stormed out of the house without saying goodbye?

Have you walked into a store, restaurant, office, someone's home and felt an avalanche of negativity? Have you been in a check-out line and the negativity surrounding the cashier literally dripped all over the place? And have you felt this negativity rub off on you? There are things you can do to ride yourself of negativity.

A shaman, recognizing negativity at the beginning of a healing session, does not tell his or her client to leave because of the negativity they are exhibiting. Reiki Master Tammy Hatherill in *When You Feel Negative Energy [12]*, tells us to "Be mindful never to promote fear." Dismissing someone reinforces low self-esteem and may contribute to the client's issues including various fears. When I meet negativity in a healing situation or in a counseling session I have the client do the following exercise along with me. I begin by saying something like this: "Let's see if we can develop an energy shift." You can do the same thing. Say out loud or to yourself, "Let's see if I can create an energy shift."

Exercise One

Clinch both hands into a fist, squeeze them tightly. Next, scrunch your face into a tight squeeze. Release. Do this twice more.

Exercise Two

Make a fist with both hands. Shove them out and away from the body. Use some force. Do this three times.

Exercise Three

Pretend to be spitting. Spit three times. Make sure you do not spit toward someone. This exercise is best done in the privacy of your home, office, or with your healer.

Exercise Four

Take a very deep breath, hold it until the count of 5, exhale very slowly. Do this three times.

Exercise Five

If you are seated, stand up. Bounce up and down five times. Slowly shake your head back and forth at the end of the fifth bounce. If you have neck issues, you may want to avoid shaking your head back and forth.

Exercise Six

Stand up, shake your booty. Do two knee bends. Yell the word *Yes.*

BIBLIOGRAPHY

Books

Atwood, Mary Dean. Spirit Healing How To Make Your Life Work. Sterling Ethos. New York. 2017

Berk, Sally Ann. *The Herb Guide*. Black Dog and Leventhal Paperbacks. New York. 1996.

Buchman, Dean Dincin, Ph.D. Ancient Healing Secrets: A Practical Guide that Works Today. Ottenchiemer Publishers, Inc. Baltimore. 1966.

Bouchardon, Patrice. *The Healing Energies of Trees*. Journey Editions. Boston. 1999.

Cunningham, Stott. *Cunningham's Encyclopedia of Magical Herbs*. Llewellyn Publications. Woodbury. 2005.

Dossey, Larry, MD. *One Mind How Our Individual Mind is Part of a Greater Consciousness and Why It Matters*. Hay House, Inc. Carlsbad. 2013.

Drake, Michael. *The Shamanic Drum A Guide to Sacred Drumming*. Talking Drums Publications. Salem, OR. 2002.

Drury, Nevill. *Shamanism*. Element. Shaftesbury. 1996.

Gerber, Richard, MD. *Vibrational Medicine, 3rd Ed.* Bear & Company. Rochester, VT. 2001.

Harner, Michael. Cave and Cosmos Shamanic Encounters with Another Reality. North Atlantic Books. Berkeley. 2013.

Horn, Gabriel(White Deer of Autumn). Spirit Drumming A Guide to the Healing Power of Rhythm. Sterling Ethos. New York. 2017.

Freke, Timothy. *Shamanic Wisdomkeepers Shamanism in the Modern World*. Godsfield Books. 1999.

Foster, Steven, and James A. Duke. *Eastern Central Medicinal Plants and Herbs*. Houghton Mifflin. Boston. 2000.

Heaven, Ross and Howard G. Charing. *Plant Spirit Shamanism*. Destiny Books. Rochester, VT. 2006.

Harner, Michael. *The Way of the Shaman*. Harper San Francisco. 1990.

Hutchens, Alma R. *Indian Herbalogy of North America*. Shambhala. Boston. 1991.

Hutchens, Alma R. *A Handbook of Native American Herbs*. Shambhala. Boston. 1992.

Ingerman, Sandra. *The Shaman's Toolkit*.Weiser Books. San Francisco. 2010.

Ingerman, Sandra. *Shamanic Journeying A Beginner's Guide*. Sounds True. Boulder. 2004.

Jenicke, Christof (ed). *PDR for Herbal Medicine 4th Edition*. Thomson Reuters Publishers. New York. 2007.

Klemp, Harold. *The Art of Spiritual Dreaming*. ECKANKAR. Minneapolis. 1999.

Lake, Medicine Grizzlybear. *Native Healer. Initiation into an Ancient Art*. Quest Books. Wheaten. 1991.

LaBerge, Stephen, Ph.D. *Lucid Dreaming*. Ballantine Books. New York. 1985.

Lennihan, Burke. RN, CCH. The Practical Herbal Medicine Handbook. Fall River Press. New York. 2014.

Mackinnon, Christa. *Shamanism Awake and Develop the Shamanic Force Within*. Hay House. Carlsbad. 2016.

Meadows, Kenneth. *Shamanic Experience A Practical Guide to Psychic Powers*. Bear & Company. Rochester, VT. 2003.

Melody. *Love is in the Earth A Kaleidoscope of Crystals* Updated. Earth-Love Publishing House. Wheat Ridge. 1997.

Mojay, Gabriel. *Aromatherapy for Healing the Spirit*. Healing Arts Press. Rochester, VT. 1997.

Pojar, Jim and Andy Mackinnon (eds). *Plants of the Pacific Northwest Coast*. Lone Pine Publishers. Redmond. 1994.

Rael, Joseph. with Mary Elizabeth Marlow. *Being & Vibration*. Council Oak Books. Tulsa. 1993.

Ridall, Kathryn, Ph.D. *Channeling How to Reach Out to Your Spirit Guides*. Bantam Books. New York. 1988.

Roman, Sanaya and Duane Packer. *Opening to Channel How to Connect with Your Guide*. H.J. Kramer, Inc. Tiburon. 1987.

Rysdyk, Evelyn. *Spirit Walking A Course in Shamanic Power*. Weiser Books. San Francisco. 2013.

Sanders, Pete A. Jr. *You Are Psychic The Free Soul Method.* A Fireside Book. New York. 1989.

Samuels, Michael, MD and Mary Rockwood Lane, Ph.D. Shaman Wisdom, Shaman Healing: Deepen Your Ability to Heal with Visionary and Spiritual Tools and Practices. John Wiley and Sons. Hoboken. 2013.

Shimer, Porter. Healing Secrets of the Native Americans. Tess Press. New York. 2004.
Smith, Kenneth. Shamanism for the Age of Science. Bear & Company. Rochester, VT. 2011.
Stack, Rick. *Out-of-Body Adventures 30 Days to the Most Exciting Experience of Your Life*. Contemporary Books. Chicago. 1988.
Tedlock, Barbara, Ph.D. *The Woman in the Shaman's Body Reclaiming the Feminine in Religion and Medicine*. Bantam Books. New York. 2006.
Tilford, Gregory L. *Edible and Medicinal Plants of the West*. Mountain Press Publishing. Missoula. 1997.
Vitebsky, Pirers. *The Shaman.* Duncan Baird Publishers. London. 1995.
Walker, Kenneth. F.R.C.S. *The Extra-Sensory Mind.* Emerson Books, Inc. New York. 1961.
Wilson, Norman W. Ph.D. *Shamanism What It's All About*. Mélange Publishing. Camano Island. 2014.
Wolf, Grey with Andy Baggott and Morning Star. *Earth Signs. How to Connect with the Natural Spirits of the Earth*. Daybreak Books. New York. 1998.

CDs

Gordon, David & Steve. Drum Medicine. 1999. Sequoia Records, Inc. Topanga.
Harner, Michael. Michael Harner's Shamanic Journey SOLO AND DOUBLE DRUMMING. 2010 The Foundation for Shamanic Studies, Inc. Command Productions. Sausalito.
Ingerman, Sandra. Shamanic Journeying. 2008. Sounds True. Boulder.

Ingerman, Sandra & Hank Wesselman. Awakening to the Spirit World. 2010.Boulder.
Llewellyn. Shamanic Journey. 2014. Paradise Music, Ltd. Naples, FL.
Meadows, Kenneth. 2003. Shamanic Experience Drumming. EQ Studios. London.
Wesselman Hank and Jill Kuykendall. Spirit Medicine Dance. 2004. Hay House. Carlsbad.

Essays by the Author [13]

Healing
Human Body Energy Fields
Is Shamanic Healing for You?
Opening Spiritual Pathways
Power Animals and Plants
Shamanic Animal Helpers
Shamanism
The Shamanic Realms Revisited
The Shamanic Spirit World
Shamanism and Time
The Shamanic World and Archetypes
What is Core Shamanism?
Seven Ways to Become a Shaman

APPENDIX ONE

List of Healing Herbs

The following chart does not list all of the herbs and their uses. Amounts to be taken are not listed. Consult your doctor before embarking upon any herbal treatment. I do not claim any degree of effectiveness for any item in the list. Caution is always the best policy. Because of its nature, the chart is located on the next page.

I strongly urge you to consult a herbalist. There is one located in Seattle, The Herbalist, in the Capitol Hill area. Cedar Mountain Herb School located in Mount Vernon, Washington offers extensive herbal training. I do not know if the owner, Susanne Jordon provides consultations.

CHART OF HERBS AND THEIR USES

NAME OF HERB	USED FOR	PARTS USED
American Elder	Headaches, colds, coughs	Root, inner bark, berries, leaves, flowers
American Linden	Indigestion	Flowers, leaves, and inner bark
Arnica	Backache, wounds, bruises, and arthritis	Flowers, roots
Bayberry	Stomach disorders	Bark, leaves, flowers
Barberry	Bladder infections	Leaves
Bloodroot	Sore throat	Rootstock
Butternut	Skin disorders	Inner bark, nuts, nut oil and leaves
Comfrey	Asthma, flu, coughs	Leaves and root
Purple Cornflower	Stings, immune system	Roots and Leaves
Goldenseal	Skin diseases, sore eyes	Roots
Horsetail	Gall stones and kidney stones	Stems

APPENDIX TWO

List of Crystals and Their Healing Uses

As with herbs, the list of crystals and their healing uses is long and varied. A caution involves the use of crystal elixirs. Don't grind up the crystal(s) and place them in water to drink. Make sure your crystals have been spiritually and physically cleansed. Be aware of the fact that some crystals will dissolve if you place them in water or get them damp. Remember, attitude, as with all healing practices, is very significant to recovery.

The chart listing crystals and what they are used for is on the next page.

CHART OF CRYSTALS AND THEIR USES

NAME OF CRYSTAL	USED FOR
Amethyst	All around good healer
Black Tourmaline	Bowel Issues
Calcite	Bone strengthener
Herkimer Diamond	Balance
Jade	Helps self-healing, stomach
Kyanite	Balancing energy
Lapis Lazuli	Releases stress
Moldavite	Spiritual healing
Opal	Pituitary Gland
Pyrite	Blocks bacteria
Quartz	Master healer, energy
Rhodonite	Calms
Selenite	Excellent blockage remover
Turquoise	Colds/flu
Unakite	Aids sleep
Vanadinte	Stimulates hormone growth
Willemite	Protects against cellular mutation

LIST OF ESSENTIAL OILS AND THEIR USES

I have discussed the value of essential oils in Chapter XII.

Because of the vast number of essential oils available, my list is short and functions as an illustration. See the Bibliography for books dealing with essential oils. The Essential Oils and Their Uses Chart is on the next page.

APPENDIX THREE

LIST OF ESSENTIAL OILS AND THEIR USES

ESSENTIAL OIL	USED FOR
Bergamot	Improves concentration
Eucalyptus	Coughs
Frankincense	Improves allergies
Ginger	Improves digestion
Grapefruit	Improves circulation
Helichrysum	Helps broken bones to heal
Lavender	Migraine headache relief
Oregano	Boosts immune system
Sage	Relieves PMS
Tea tree	Blisters
Thieves Oil	Immune system
Umbellularia californica Leaf	Relief of nasal congestion
Valerian	Induces sleep
Wintergreen	Arthritis relief
Yarrow Leaf	Stops bleeding
Zedoary Bark	Anxiety relief

APPENDIX FOUR

The gentleman who made my rattle and who also makes drums is Randy Two-Eagles Billings. A picture of his handmade rattle appears on page 29 and of his drums appears on page 31. In terms of his interest in drums, Randy says, "I have always heard the beating Heart of the Great Mother Earth and dreamt many times of the Buffalo. Such dreams have had a great influence on the creation of my drums, rattles, and dream catchers and walking sticks. Shown here is Randy with some of his drums.

You can connect with Randy at his Face Book page by using the "message" system: https://www.facebook.com/randy.billings.73 or you can e-mail him at guilliverbill@yahoo.com.

CONCLUSION

It is and has been my abiding hope that we human beings include some of the workable and successful healing lessons of our ancestors into our modern healing practices. Unfortunately, we have a tendency to romanticize our past histories. The old sayings of "you can't go home again" or "you can't step in the same creek water more than once" do not mean that there aren't things of our past that are of value and they can and should be brought forward. If these ancient healing techniques were so bad, none of us would be here today. The human race would have been the extinct species.

I sincerely hope the information provided in this little book brings you some understanding of what a shaman does and opens the door to you for other healing possibilities; and that it has removed any of the personal concerns or fears you might have about shamanic healing.

Namaste,
Norman

ABOUT THE AUTHOR

Dr. Wilson has a Ph.D. in the humanities and one in metaphysical humanism. He is a spiritual counselor, minister, and a retired educator. Wilson is a certified Master Reiki Healer, Level Three with advanced certification in Usui Shiki Ryoho System of Natural Healing. He is the author of over a dozen books and nearly 500 articles published on the Internet. His training in shamanism began when he was seven years old.

FOOTNOTES

(identified in the text by square brackets)

[1] Reprinted with author's permission. *Shamanism What It's All About*. Mélange Publishing. Camano Island. 2014, p12.

[2] Refers to that instantaneous intuitive connection between minds as rationalized by Bell's Theorem, the Principle of Non-Locality in Quantum Physics. This is not unlike Jung's archetypes and his collective unconscious.

[3] The few photos I have of the Baskatong days do not include any of Elisapie. The large hampers full of scrapbooks containing thousands of photos I no longer have. Those were stored in a family member's home and the person who inherited it apparently felt no need to keep them. It saddens.

[4] Harner is the author of *The Way of the Shaman* (Harper Row, 1980) and *Cave and Cosmos* (North Atlantic Books, 2013).

[5] In some of my writings I said my parents were at my initiation ceremony. I did that because I did not want to give the impression I was neglected, shuttled off, so to speak. They were privy to the gifts I had received, bow and arrows, for example.

[6] Lake Medicine Grizlybear (Bobby Lake-Thom). *Native Healer Initiation into an Ancient Art*. Wheaton, Ill. Quest Books, 1991, p. 41.

[7] Talking Drum Publications. Salem. Revised Edition. 2009. p,18.

[8] Often climate makes a leather drum difficult to keep in tune, especially for those of us who live in the Northwest of the United States.

[9] Because of the climate in which I live, I have chosen a non-animal skin drum and because of my concern for animals. My original drum, given away many years ago was of animal skin.

[10] Students were all eighteen years of age or older. They were given the opportunity to opt out of the demonstration. One did.

[11] I deliberately keep the prayer short because the healing session is a set length of time, generally no more than an hour.

[12] Published in Reiki Rays, February 18, 2016.

[13] With nearly 500 essays published, those that are listed are just a sample. They are available on the Internet, especially EzineArticles.com.

www.ingramcontent.com/pod-product-compliance
Ingram Content Group UK Ltd.
Pitfield, Milton Keynes, MK11 3LW, UK
UKHW020223250726
13967UKWH00001B/166

9 781786 951632